BUSTA RHYME

*I SHUFFLE THROUGH MY MIND
TO SEE IF I CAN FIND
THE WORDS I LEFT BEHIND*
- GREEN DAY

EXPRESSIONS OF YOUTH

Edited By Warren Arthur

First published in Great Britain in 2017 by:

YoungWriters Est. 1991

Young Writers
Remus House
Coltsfoot Drive
Peterborough
PE2 9BF
Telephone: 01733 890066
Website: www.youngwriters.co.uk

All Rights Reserved
Book Design by Spencer Hart
© Copyright Contributors 2017
SB ISBN 978-1-78820-309-8
Printed and bound in the UK by BookPrintingUK
Website: www.bookprintinguk.com
YB0333QY

FOREWORD

Welcome, Reader, to 'Busta Rhyme – Expressions Of Youth'.

For Young Writers' latest poetry competition, we asked our writers to wow us with their words and bust out their bard side!

The result is this collection of fantastic poetic verse that covers a whole host of different topics. Get ready to be blown away by these passionate poems about love and relationships, school and bullying, equality and human rights, and demanding day-to-day issues that come with living in today's society. This collection has a poem to suit everyone.

Whereas the majority of our writers chose to express themselves with a free verse style, others gave themselves the challenge of other techniques such as acrostics and rhyming couplets.

There was a great response to this competition which is always nice to see, and the standard of entries was excellent, therefore I'd like to say a big thank you and well done to everyone who entered.

Warren Arthur

CONTENTS

Independent Entries

Alexander John Cairns (13)	1
Daniel Thompson	2
Romiya Sahota (11)	4

Alcester Grammar School, Alcester

Molly Elizabeth Roberts	6
Abi Collett (13)	8
Ben Robinson	9
Sakshi Rajeev (12)	10
Oliver James Parriss (13)	11

Aston University Engineering Academy, Birmingham

Lara Scrivens (15)	12
Kaleem Riaz (16)	13
Sandeep Kaur (16)	14
Ventsislav Milkov (16)	15

Birchfield Independent Girls' School, Aston

Navaira Mehmood	16
Hawa Ali (14)	18
Aishah Maryam Smith (13)	20
Maymuna Madihah (13)	21
Rumaisa Ahmed (13)	22
Suad Ahmed (13)	24
Nazmin Ali (13)	25
Sabiha Islam (14)	26

Braybrook Centre, Parkfields

William Dixon (13)	27

Cambourne Village College, Cambourne

Orlando James	28

Cambridge Regional College, Cambridge

Progression Garden Class	30
Hannah Reed (21)	31

Chase House School, Brownhills

J O (13)	32
B L (12)	33
C B-C (11)	34
J F (14)	35

Handsworth Wood Girls' Academy, Birmingham

Amy Brueton	36
Mariya Hussain (11)	39
Sophia Eesha Kaur (15)	40
Henna Najib (12)	43
Huda Ali (12)	44
Alisha Safdar (12)	45
Javiaria (12) & Nafeesa Islam	46

Higham Lane School Business And Enterprise College, Nuneaton

Izzy Bromage (12)	47
Louis Salmon (13)	48
Jessica Bond (13)	49
Sky Paige Duffy (12)	50

Holte School, Lozells

Terenso Cunningham (13)	51
Reanna Dixon-Scott (13)	52

King Solomon International Business School, Birmingham

Kanye Mitchell (12)	54
Lily Wilson (13)	56
Kristan Aaliyah Alex Hines (13)	58
Dibora Hadish (13)	60
Ashan Mills (13)	61
Lauren Edmeade (13)	62
Aneika Cooper (13)	63
Ludan Alawad (13)	64
Zaynah Begum (13)	65

Litcham School, Litcham

Caitlin Millington (13)	66
Liberty Blackmore (13)	68
Felix Platt (12)	70
Conner Curson (15)	73
Ada Everett (13)	74
Georgina Denney (13)	76
Amelia Platt (15)	78
Charles Crook (13)	79
Jack Raby (13)	80
Bayley Able (13)	82
Caleb Bower (13)	84
Alysha Jolie West (13)	86
Dominic Hancock (13)	87
Sian Freestone (13)	88
Isaac Bower (13)	89
Sophia Louise Djiakouris (13)	90

Simon (12)	91
Danielle Mia Harrowing (13)	92
Ben Wilson (12)	93
Sophie Adelaide Stangroom (13)	94
Ella Westhorpe (13)	96
Evelyn Scott (13)	97
Scarlett Stevens (13)	98
Millie Fisher (13)	99
Amber Hayden (12)	100
Jessica Elizabeth Edwards (12)	101
Danny Benson (13)	102
Levi List (13)	103
Katie Duthie (13)	104
Megan Day (14)	105
Boe Wilcox (13)	106
Caitlin Hawkins	107

Meole Brace School Science College, Shrewsbury

Artin Shey (15)	108
Jade Hamilton (13)	110
Chloe Marie Unwin	112
Jade Chloe Cox (15)	114
Ciara Lucas-Garner (12)	115
Robbie Richards (13)	116
Matthew James Cumming (13)	117
Owen Sadd (13)	118
James Adcock (15)	119
Aidan Blake (14)	120

Ormiston Denes Academy, Lowestoft

Ethan Mark Provis (12)	121
Abigail Crame (12)	122
George Richard Eric Sibbald (11)	123
Kelsey Earp (11)	124

Pakefield High School, Lowestoft

Jea Franks (12)	125

Leanne (11), Ellie Beenham, Evie & Rosie Elizabeth Graham	126
Rachel Louise Sewell (13)	128
Chloe Rose Jacobs (12)	129
Tabitha Bond (13)	130
Kelsey Leech (13)	131
Amelia Gow (12)	132
Molly Bullard (13)	133
Trinity Meadez (13)	134
Jack James Jefferies (13)	135
Amber Hill (13)	136
Xander Dennis (13)	137

Sandwell Community School - Wednesbury Campus, Hydes Road

Bradley Garratt (13)	138
Cameron Martin (13)	139
Connor Harper (12)	140

Seaford College, Petworth

Charlotte Upcott (11)	141
Marcus Fairweather (14)	142
Toby Loeffen-Ames (14)	144
Ella Kuchanny (14)	146
Tom Jillians (14)	148
Lottie Amy Hubbard (14)	150
Rafe Ernest Nisbet (12)	151
Alfie Wakefield (14)	152
Helena Mitchinson (11)	153
Grace Clark (12)	154
Amy Styles (11)	155
Charlotte Brinsmead (12)	156
Tom Thornton (12)	157
Lewis Fox (14)	158
Tabitha Hill (14)	159
Molly Holt (12)	160
Benjamin Cotton (12)	161
Lola Andrews (11)	162
Daisy Bassett (14)	163
Henry McMorran (14)	164
Mandy Rabina (12)	165

Abbie Biggs (12)	166

St Clements High School, King's Lynn

Charly Peter Spurge (12)	167
Jasmine Elise Chapman (11)	168
Madison Angel Rudd (11)	171

Stanground Academy, Stanground

Alex Ubakanma (13)	172
Daniel Read (14)	174
Cameron (13)	175
Skye Chapman (12)	176
Kenya Renshaw (13)	178
Brandon Green (13)	179
Megan Cunningham (13)	180
Toby Lusher (12)	181
Megan Shire (13)	182
Sam Cannizzaro (13)	183
Robbie Dowland (13)	184
Maisie Jean Goodley (13)	185
Bethany Perry (13)	186
Jessica Bowman (12)	187
Oliwia Wiktoria Sliwinska (12)	188
Jenesis Smoot (13)	189
Alicia Gilbert (13)	190
Casey Sexton (12)	191
William Lee Guy (13)	192
Sam Bunczik (13)	193

Thomas Adams School, Wem

Jack Gourlay (13)	194
Evelyn Ross Platt (14)	196
Charlotte Francis (13)	198
JJ Udy (12)	199
Freya Davies (13)	200
Ben Gwilliam (13)	201
Catherine Sutton (13)	202

THE POEMS

Untitled

The Earth trembled and the kingdom fell,
Prince of Morocco was angry, 'Welcome to Hell'.
Lorenzo was fortunate but Shylock was not.
Little Jessica ran away, left his heart in a tied-up knot.

Alexander John Cairns (13)

The Future

What do you think is going to happen
If we carry on this way?
We see another day,
The world is being treated very badly,
It's not fair,
We need to care.
Without animals we have nothing.
Like bees,
Without them,
There will be flowers dead everywhere,
Just towers of them.
What about tigers?
They need a home, their nest,
They are not pests.
Stop destroying their homes.
What did they do to you?
And phones,
Give it to a friend,
A family member,
Someone in need of it!
Don't chuck it away,
I bet you don't know where it goes.
All I know is it turns to waste,
Puffs of black smoke.

What if the world ended?
It's crazy to think about,
I mean, think about it for a long time,
It's strange!
There would be nothing,
No us, no wildlife, plants or animals.
What would happen?
Have I changed your opinion on the world?
Start caring, don't litter,
Let the world get fitter.

Daniel Thompson

A Magical World

In my dream,
I'm in a new world with magical creatures,
And no teachers,
Walking as slow as a snail,
I could see the fluffy clouds underneath me,
Closing in on me.

In my dream,
I could see a soft, white rabbit,
I looked up,
To see a scorching, shimmering sun,
What a lot of fun.

In my dream,
I was a quiet mouse
About to pounce.

In my dream,
A unicorn danced with jewellery,
Up and down pouncing around,
About to give me a pound,
With fur the colour pink,
About to think.

In my dream,
Above the emerald-green trees
Lay stars in a galaxy
Not far from the mighty dragon,
Who breathed fire.

Romiya Sahota (11)

Anger And Hiding Your Feelings Poem

Anger is red,
A scorching flame,
The fuse of a bomb,
Meant to maim.

It seeps in through the windows,
Floods all the floor,
Fills up the room,
Explodes through the doors.

Ticking down the seconds until vicious outburst
And, finally, the world downpours in molten rain.

Hiding emotions is black,
Alone, but in control,
The world slipping away,
A swelling, drowning soul.

Inside there is shrill screaming,
A battle of loss and fear,
A path to self-destruction,
Your fate imminent and clear.

As the seconds tick by until silence, at last,
And the world crumbles from hopeless restrain.

At least anger can have an end,
Although burning bright,
Dies to an ember.
The arms of depression, therefore,
Are infinitely worse;
All hope is gone after darkness invades.

Molly Elizabeth Roberts
Alcester Grammar School, Alcester

Coward

You think you're all that for posting a message,
But you're too scared to show your face and you could've just left it.
Do you really know that person? Or how they feel?
For you it may be a joke,
But for them it's all too real.

Behind a computer screen, safe in your bubble,
Just a few words cause heartbreaking trouble.
Well done - for five minutes you look cool to your mates,
But for the innocent you've targeted, it could be too late.

Abi Collett (13)
Alcester Grammar School, Alcester

Anger Poem

Hiding your feelings
Piles them inside
You think that it helps
But in you reside
Feelings of anger
And horrible fire
Yet sweet revenge
Is all you desire
Using these feelings
You've never showed
You start to crack
And eventually explode
Using this sadness
That made you feel meek
You throw out your fist
And pummel the weak.

Ben Robinson
Alcester Grammar School, Alcester

Hiding Your Feelings

Pain, anger, sadness,
No one knows how I feel.
A constant battle with my mind
And nothing seems to heal.
A body filled with darkness,
Even in the light of day.
A mouth filled with so many words,
But never a chance to say.
With a soul of eternal silence,
But that's how it goes.
To have to hide your feelings every day
And no one ever knows.

Sakshi Rajeev (12)
Alcester Grammar School, Alcester

Anger

Anger,
Holding in an ear-piercing scream,
The loss of your favourite football team,
Anger,
Hate,
Stop, it's not too late,
Anger, stop,
Violence,
Don't sit in silence,
Anger, stop,
Don't hold it in, let it go,
Anger is not the way to go,
Open the bottle, set it free,
Keep your head up and be happy.

Oliver James Parriss (13)
Alcester Grammar School, Alcester

This Book
(Based on Lara's emotions, while reading 'Thirteen Reasons Why')

'It's a lie what they say,'
You tell yourself as you lay
Each night on your bed,
Recalling the words that *they* said.

They don't see the sorrow,
The fear of no tomorrow
And when the pain becomes too much
It's onto life you must clutch.

Don't they know that what they say,
It can affect you in this way?
The image of self-hate,
Invites itself onto the plate.

The thoughts become stronger
And the days become longer.
The pain won't go away,
You feel like it's your final day.

And your soul, now broken, slips out of your wrists
You hope in some way, on some day you'll be missed.

Lara Scrivens (15)
Aston University Engineering Academy, Birmingham

You Make Me Laugh

You make me laugh when I cry
You make me love when I want to die
You make me smile when I want to frown
You then turn my life upside down
You believe in me when no one else does.

You're my now, my is, and my was
When you call my name I begin to blush
I'm afraid that people will notice I need you so much
When I'm with you time flies so fast
It's like the present is in the past.

I need you more than you can believe
I love you more than you can conceive
I hope that my life will stay this way
Because I wouldn't have it any other way.

Kaleem Riaz (16)
Aston University Engineering Academy, Birmingham

A Sad Film

I feel sorrow
because what she did was full of horror.
I couldn't believe what I heard
because I was sad for her son,
he should have run.

I tried,
I tried to make myself understand,
why did she do that to her own?
She injured his bones,
she made him cry,
cold as stones.

Sandeep Kaur (16)
Aston University Engineering Academy, Birmingham

Roses Are Candy

Roses are red
Violets are blue
I bought too much candy
But so did you.

I ate all my share
You got very sad
You said it's not fair
Your candy was all bad.

You complained to Mom
That it was my fault
I spent all my money
From my now empty vault.

Ventsislav Milkov (16)
Aston University Engineering Academy, Birmingham

Don't Know

Yo!
I have a dream to be the one I wanna be,
The one I see upon the screen,
That's the one I wanna be,
But dem people,
They always talkin',
But I'm just gonna keep on walkin',
They think I'm a wannabe,
But they don't know,
They don't know,
They don't know the real me, the true me,
The me that I wanna be and I'm gonna be,
The me that I was destined to be.
They say you're too young to know what's good fun for you,
Too young to do what's best for you,
They say you're too young, too young, too young.
They think I'm always lying,
Just sitting in the corner crying,
But there's just no denying,
The fact that I'm never gonna give up,
I'm just gonna keep trying.
Cos it's a new age and now I've got a new name,
Now I'm gonna be the real me, the true me,
The me that I wanna be.

The me that I'm gonna be, the me that I was destined to be
And they just don't know, they don't know,
They don't know me.
Navaira Mehmood
Birchfield Independent Girls' School, Aston

Escape

I ran with my heart going *pound*,
Fear running round and round,
No looking side to side,
Just the motto, 'run and hide'.

The men had rock hearts
As they pushed me into their carts.
They ran at the speed of lightning,
It was absolutely frightening.

They locked the door and told me to stay,
They told me not to run away,
I said no, I wanted to go,
But they kept me back anyway.

My hands and toes turned ice-cold,
The walls around me on them were mould,
As soon as they left me all alone,
The way of escape shone.

The alarms rang,
The guns went *bang*,
I was done, I was gone,
I was nothing but a memory,
They knew I was temporary.

I ran with my heart going *pound*,
Fear running round and round,
No looking side to side,
Just the motto, 'run and hide'.

Hawa Ali (14)
Birchfield Independent Girls' School, Aston

Trapped

I don't know where we went wrong,
fine one minute, broken the next
though the impact hit me the most you were OK without me
because you had the upper hand, controlled me in every possible way
we had a stronger bond than anyone could imagine
you were closer to me than my jugular vein,
always in my thoughts and it broke just like that...

you left in peace, left me in pieces though
couldn't breathe, I was trapped
every time I saw you on the streets I'd turn and run
my anxiety always got the better of me
couldn't even cross the road some days, wanted the earth to swallow me up like I'd never even existed at all
then I remembered you weren't real... it was my insecurities the whole time
I was fighting a battle with my own soul.

Aishah Maryam Smith (13)
Birchfield Independent Girls' School, Aston

Alone

Me and the emptiness
The big black, unfilled hole inside my heart.
All alone
The words which sends chills down my spine,
Looking for something that I can call mine.
I look at other people laughing together
Knowing it's just me all alone forever.
I'm trying to cure my own heartache
but there's not much more I can take.
I have to accept that it's just me,
all alone forever
Even with everybody around me
I still feel like it's only me
All alone forever.

Maymuna Madihah (13)
Birchfield Independent Girls' School, Aston

Alone

Sitting alone in a dark room,
Waiting and waiting,
But no one came.

The next day, the same thing,
All I could hear was the clock,
Tick, tick, tick.

Scared no one would come,
Just me alone,
Would anyone ever come?

Feeling isolated,
Feeling worried,
Feeling scared.

Still waiting,
Would anyone ever come?

Finally the door creaked open,
Finally someone came,
Finally I found a friend.

She came and sat by me,
I'd found a best friend,
I was not alone any more.

I had a best friend,
She smiled and hugged me,
She said, 'Everything's going to be OK,
I'm here!'

Rumaisa Ahmed (13)
Birchfield Independent Girls' School, Aston

Stand Up

In a dark room,
In cold sheets,
I can't feel a single thing,
I lost myself in my heart,
The medicine is to fix my head.

You know I'd rather be alone,
But you keep calling me on the phone,
The actions of my heart,
I can't say no,
It's tearing me apart,
You make it hard to let you go.

You tie my hand behind my back,
You torture me without no lack,
I finally stand up
And you fall down,
I am the one now with the crown.

Suad Ahmed (13)
Birchfield Independent Girls' School, Aston

Your Lies Are Bullets

Your mouth's a gun,
your tongue is the sharpest of swords,
there's an ache in your absence.
No war in anger has ever put out a fire before lightning,
remember that next time you're fighting
In the town where I was born in.

'Every breathe you take,
every move you make,
every bond you make, every step you take, I'll be watching you.'

Nazmin Ali (13)
Birchfield Independent Girls' School, Aston

Doom

In a day so dark
A wolf lets out a howl
A distant bark
The taste of fear, so foul.

How I thought it was fine
The screams and tears
Sending shivers up my spine
Scatter, the creature is near.

If only we could get far away,
But it's too late, *crash, boom!*
If only it was today
We would not have met our doom.

Sabiha Islam (14)
Birchfield Independent Girls' School, Aston

iPhone

iPhone with my friends and family
iPhone easily and willingly

iPhone in the night and day
iPhone allows me to play

iPhone has a finger scanner
iPhone doesn't display a banner

iPhone can store many memories
iPhone has many accessories

iPhone simply the best
iPhone can't be put to rest.

William Dixon (13)
Braybrook Centre, Parkfields

Atomi

It streaks across the sky,
leaving behind the white trail of a plane,
Time just slows down and I watch
from the front row seat of my personal disaster movie
as the thing I fear the most falls miles away.

For some, I hear screaming,
a long, sharp, ear-piercing,
expression of the sheer agony.
For others, it is silence,
the lonely crushing guilt of
years of disappointment and tragedy.

I am unique in the final scene of my life,
I laugh at the hilarity of the situation.
This is like one of the comics I wrote when I was younger,
the only difference being that there are no heroes,
no specific divide between good and evil,
no care for the innocent.

I curse as the masses around me glare at me,
don't they understand?
Nothing matters any more!
The memories of those happy days
will comfort me in my final seconds.

In a few short moments,
I am transported to my infancy,
my childhood,
the time I stored model after model
of Lego in that storage cabinet.
My first crush,
My first job.

My thoughts turn to my family,
how will they respond to my death?
Will they have a difficult life in the new age?
Are they safe?

And then I am back in the present,
sitting on the bonnet of my car,
In the last act of my drastic play,
I drink the remaining can of beer.

Then the world is turned orange and black:
the atomic bomb detonates over the city.
I close my eyes and continue to laugh,
this time with a hint of sadness.
Turns out the thing you hate your entire life,
will always find you in the end.
A breeze slides down the street,
and carries me away.

Orlando James
Cambourne Village College, Cambourne

Winter's Progression

W orld of
I ce, a
N est in the
T ree. The
E volution of the
R obin rests in the branches

W hat
O blivion!
N atural
D ecorations
E verywhere. A
R evolution that
L asts
A ll
N ight in
D arkness.

Progression Garden Class
Cambridge Regional College, Cambridge

Untitled

Our days are grey
The sky is grey
My hair is grey.

The trees are green
The grass is green
Some bins are green.

Some days are grey
I mean to say
Long live the Queen.

Hannah Reed (21)
Cambridge Regional College, Cambridge

Your Mind

Your head works in many different ways, our last argument replays
Over and over in my mind, keeps me awake at night
The mind must be master of the body
The mind has a will of its own
The mind stops me sleeping at night
I fought and I fought but my mind just kept running away
I tried to hide from it but it just kept coming back
The more I run the more I start to die inside
Do I fight it or do I put up with it?
Somebody help me,
Everyone is ignoring me, what do I do?
The heart fights to keep me alive
The mind and the heart work together
You told me we were going to be forever
'Til death do us part.

J O (13)
Chase House School, Brownhills

Mortally Betrayed

M ad at certain people.
O bviously people don't know what I am thinking or feel.
R epeatedly angry.
T errified of what's going to happen.
A nger is getting worse.
L eave me alone.
L eave me alone!
Y es, what do you want

B eing betrayed is horrible.
E moji faces near.
T ripping up on your own feet.
R aindrops are like tears.
A nyone please help.
Y ell at the top of my lungs.
E motions are running.
D ance, dance, I just want to get my feelings out.

B L (12)
Chase House School, Brownhills

Anti-Bullying

Please Mister Bully, don't make me cry,
Punch me again and you'll be punching the sky.

You kick me, squeeze me, throw me to the ground,
You know I'm in care but I'll soon come round.

I'll get bigger, faster and stronger than you,
I'll try to be your friend and you could too.

I know I always try to oppose you,
It's not just you, it's what I always do.

Now I'm older people make bad choices,
We don't have to maybe, it's life?

Maybe you could choose...
'Choose life, not war'.

C B-C (11)
Chase House School, Brownhills

The Poem

Why does a poem have to rhyme?
Why does a poem have beats in time?
Why does a poem have to be strange?
Why does a poem have to work in a range?
Why does a poem need work and sound?
Why does a poem need to be in a book and bound?
Why does a poem make me feel sad?
Why does a poem make me feel bad?
Why does a poem have to be so dramatic?
Why does a poem make me feel frantic?

J F (14)
Chase House School, Brownhills

assion For Love

Paints all lined in unison,
Cutting alone on a dusty frame,
Bright colours greying and hard,
Fibres of dust fluttering in the bright light,
Pictures ripped or covered with neglect,
Poems, all that I resist to repeat,
Darkness arose and dust fell lightly
Over the dismay of the room,
A forgotten place,
Old tunes lingered in the air,
So quietly,
One picture stuck out in my line of sight,
The paper ripped lightly by each end,
The paper yellowing from the dust and hostility,
A heart, a red bloody sunk heart,
Being ripped in half,
Pulled from its other side,
Blood drips deadly out of its shell,
I looked away,
Seeing more dust form,
More darkness arose,
So I closed my eyes,
Ready to be forgotten,
My work dusty and broken,
Forgotten

Until a hand cupped tightly to mine,
Stroking my knuckles,
Lovingly,
I opened my dull eyes,
Staring at honey-brown
Bright eyes,
I see a girl,
Her hair rested on her shoulders,
she smelled wonderful,
She whispered sweet
Nothings in my ears,
Saying, love yourself,
Enjoy, be happy,
Forget everyone,
Slowly promising my old, dusty paints
So I stood after so long,
And began to cover all
My love with paints,
I wrote until my hand ached,
Listened longingly to my old tunes,
I felt myself being pulled closer!
Looking at the picture!
Saw not long ago
And fixed at,
A heart,
A whole heart,
And a shell to protect it

The girl smiled and I felt
Glee in my lungs,
My passion had rose,
I had a passion,
A passion for her,
I had poems for love,
And painting for love,
I had a passion for love.

Amy Brueton
Handsworth Wood Girls' Academy, Birmingham

I Have A Little Sister

I have a little sister called Layla,
She is really cute and funny,
She really likes her toy bunny,
I have a little sister,
She is my little princess, my queen, my friend, my life,
She is an angel (sometimes),
You may think she is really good,
But sometimes she can be a cheeky monkey,
She screams when I talk to anyone,
She tries to get me in trouble!
Back onto the adorable side of her,
She tries to make me laugh when I'm sad,
She knows how to do the animal sounds.
'What does a cow say?'
'Moooo!'
What does a goose say?'
'Spits!'
'Do you love me?'
'No!'
I have a little sister who I will always love
And look out for, no matter what!
I love you Layla!

Mariya Hussain (11)
Handsworth Wood Girls' Academy, Birmingham

Questions...

Do you ever give up?
All that seems to happen is you breaking down,
Not once or twice though;
Maybe a couple of times.

Does it get better?
Questioning all night and day.
But all that seems to get out
Is silent sobs.

Can they hear me?
My thoughts are beating out my brain
Trying to hammer its way out,
Into the open.

Will I ever be the same again?
Happy, is what I used to be.
Now the days just seem to get darker
There's literally no escape.

I could just end it all right?
Once and for all.
But that's no good,
To anyone at all.

Can't they feel my pain?
They say they understand.
Maybe they're just sympathetic,
But I don't need sympathy.

Can't they see what it is doing to me?
It's tiring me out;
Physically, mentally and
Emotionally.

I want it to end.
I want to go away,
Far, far away
And never to be seen again.

I just want the chance
To be happy again.
To be the little girl
I never really got to be.

All my life has shown is:
Hurt, sorrow and pain.
A few happy days -
It never lasts though - nothing ever does.

For some reason life always hits me
Right in the face with something new
Something new to face
But I can't handle no more.

I just feel I want to jump.
Jump off the rails.
Or fly into the Land of Freedom

I just want to live
And not feel dead inside,
Is that so hard?

Sophia Eesha Kaur (15)
Handsworth Wood Girls' Academy, Birmingham

Art

Art, it allows me to escape into my own world of creativity,
Full of imagination and no negativity,
Each intricate stroke of paint composed by a brush is beautiful in its own way,
Each sketch so detailed, it blows my mind away,
The blend of two colours creates an ambience perceived by the human eye,
All different techniques to apply,
Colours, all unique and of all different shades,
Blended on a canvas as the colours slowly fade,
It can take months to produce a piece of art,
After that, one shall feel proud, that feeling will reside deep down in your heart,
Art is a perfect way to express your opinion and view,
The creator of your masterpiece is you.

Henna Najib (12)
Handsworth Wood Girls' Academy, Birmingham

Fruit, Glorious Fruit

Apricots, strawberries, mangoes galore,
Oranges, bananas, foods I adore.
Juicy and fruity, words not enough,
To explain my love of my favourites.

Why don't I hate them like other kids?
Hate them like Rosie and little, silly Sid?
Am I a tad weird for liking these delights?
For I truly don't know if I'm wrong or right.

I wish I could tell you; I'm perfect and pure,
But any of those words, I'm not sure.
Do stop pestering, I'll now have to shoot,
For I'm tempted to tell you the secret of fruit.

Huda Ali (12)
Handsworth Wood Girls' Academy, Birmingham

Animals

A nimals, my friends, are the best things ever
N ever let them leave as they are the most precious things in my life
I n my house I long to see animals there for me to fill with glee
M y favourites are cats, dogs, wolves and foxes
A ll of them I long to have
L ong to see all over the land
S ome in water, some in the air but I don't need a bird nest in my hair!

Alisha Safdar (12)
Handsworth Wood Girls' Academy, Birmingham

Eternal Youth

2400 thousand days and 4300 nights,
An eternal youth that will shine
Throughout the dreadful day and night.
One day at a time, one moment shall survive.
Now I lay, time to rest.
As I place my head down
And so what I no longer detest,
Holding you close up to me inside.
I will live on, however no longer in sight.
Before I go I wish you goodbye.
I will see you sometime after July.

Javiaria (12) & Nafeesa Islam
Handsworth Wood Girls' Academy, Birmingham

A Dream

Awakening from my deep sleep,
Trying to recall my dream,
But knowing it would never keep,
A better reality, lost it would seem.

Would I...
Swim in the largest ocean,
Drink from a magical potion,
Be a character in my favourite book
Or be a world-famous chef and cook?

Awakening from deep sleep,
Trying to recall my dream,
But knowing it would never keep,
A worse reality, lost it would seem.

Would I...
Fall into a world full of horror,
Die a gruesome death tomorrow,
Eat an apple that's gone bad
Or live in a world where everyone is sad?

Awakening from a deep sleep,
Trying to recall my dream,
But knowing it would never keep
A reality, either good or bad, lost it would seem...

Izzy Bromage (12)
Higham Lane School Business And Enterprise College, Nuneaton

My Brother

Like sweet and sour
A nightmare and a happy dream
A hero and a villain
The fox and rabbit.

He comes and goes like a distant memory
As close as clothes
As far away as a galaxy
That's my brother alright.

There to bail me out
Although he was the one who caused it
He loaned me money
Although he made me broke.

I was the olive tree
He was the pear tree
One hated
One loved.

These pictures seem to be now fiction
But it's fiction
Just two boys
Looking for some oil.

Louis Salmon (13)
Higham Lane School Business And Enterprise College, Nuneaton

What Does Earth Look Like?

What does Earth look like from another star?
Is it beautiful and perfect
Or is it just an ugly scar?
Are they up there in the dark?
Do they have tails or look like a shark?
Does thinking about us make them spark?
As we cut down trees
And pollute our seas,
Destroy the wild and kill the bees.
Are we monsters in their eyes?
Making chaos from hurt and lies
As they watch from the skies.

Jessica Bond (13)
Higham Lane School Business And Enterprise College, Nuneaton

Space

Space is colourful,
Galaxies are blue,
The moon looks like a big pot of glue,
The sun will burn
And stars will turn.
Clouds are white
Like big marshmallows in the sky.
Jupiter is red,
Saturn is blue,
Pluto is up high,
Floating around the sky.

Sky Paige Duffy (12)
Higham Lane School Business And Enterprise College, Nuneaton

My World, My Life, My Poem

I love my neighbourhood
I love the people as I should.
The people I chill with are so good
But I don't hang with falsehood.
Some people want to take my ground
So my mom tells me to watch around.
I know my morals, I know where I stand.
My goal is to win the grand.

I've got friends that are true.
We are friends but you don't know what we've been through.
We always stick together.
Our friendship will never ever be soft like leather.
We have no boss, as we said.
If there are any problems we're always one step ahead.
I don't want to say any more, you already know.
All I'm saying is our friendship will never blow.

My family is so strong.
We have a good friendship because we always bond.
I love my family and they love me.
My parents adore me I can guarantee.
My parents, they don't like lying.
Our love will never be dying.
This is the end of my poem
Now that I have spoken.

Terenso Cunningham (13)
Holte School, Lozells

My Pain

My situation does not define who I am
I define who I am.
Just because I have problems and issues
Doesn't mean you always have to show me
Sympathy and tell me what you would do
If you were in my shoes.

Just because I cry myself to sleep at night
Doesn't mean that you always need to ask me if I'm alright.
Just because when I look in the mirror I don't like what I see
Doesn't mean that I don't know who I'm supposed to be.

See I don't know what I did to deserve this life.
But I must've messed up real bad because
Every day of my life is a fight.
A fight for survival and it's even
Harder when you're suicidal.

You wake up every day and question your existence
You try to talk to someone for help but no one listens.

You wish and you pray but it never seems to work.
You think to yourself, *Wow, is this all I'm worth?*

See nobody would care if I left this cruel world today
Because all I'm doing here is simply filling up space.

I feel like I'm worth nothing and have no reason to be here.
I wish this could all just end and I'd disappear.

But let's be real
Our wishes never come true
If they did then I'd be happy and maybe even pretty too.

Reanna Dixon-Scott (13)
Holte School, Lozells

I Broke News

They say 'breaking news'
But news isn't broken
They're building headlines
But the headlines
Aren't constructed
Donald Trump makes it because you were stupid
People falling apart - call it reverse Cupid
Jamaica falling apart, war in the Ukraine
Let's fix the walls that brought pain

Multiple nations making bombs
But not knowing where the resources come from
So if the news is always broken
Let's fix it with the words commonly spoken

Breaking news! Multiple countries poor
Nations are so blind it's like an open door
Of man-made disasters, nuke testing
Have I just broke news?

Like a book, it's open, pending
Recommending
And comprehension
Is filling up our heads with nonsense. Nonsense,
Constructing in our minds.

Before we turn on the TV,
I broke news
And I'm happy.
Kanye Mitchell (12)
King Solomon International Business School, Birmingham

Invisible

'Stop!' you yell
'Stop what?' I ask

All I ever do is tell you how I feel,
I wish you would engage.
I long to even hear your rage
What I would do to hear
Even your angry tones

All I get is shut down.
Looked over.
Ignored with a capital 'I'.

Your cold, half-hearted glare,
Your sigh of deep despair
I am forgotten before I am even seen

Forgotten like your mother's birthday
Dropped like a bad date
I am but an error in your eyes

I'm just a bug in your world's script:
A blot on your map
A hole in your trousers.

At best, an irritation
At worst, I am not I.
Now I am simply, painfully, horribly
Invisible.

I was a person but I am no more
I breathe but I do not live
You ask me to stop, yet

I have barely begun.

Lily Wilson (13)
King Solomon International Business School, Birmingham

Smoking Is Bad

You can't find the money to pay your bills
Because you spent it all on
Cigars, cigarettes.

You can't pay for food for your family
You can't take your family out to
Cinemas, restaurants or fun places

You end up broke,
End up sick, weak, unable to be yourself.
Can't bear watching your loved ones seeing you sick
Unable to function.

Stop smoking or your loved ones
Will have to see you suffer
Unable to breathe, watching you die.

No child should watch their father die
Slowly, right in front of them.

You - unable to do anything.

Smoking is bad
Effective and irrelevant
Life-threatening
Ruining people's lives and children's minds
Hopefully you'll listen to the signs
Cancer kills.

You fade away

Smoking is bad
Effective and irrelevant.

Kristan Aaliyah Alex Hines (13)
King Solomon International Business School, Birmingham

Stop!

Stop!
Don't cut yourself, you're not paper
Broken mirror
Bleeding fist
It's hard to see you suffer.

Stop!
Don't hide your face, you're not ugly
Sleeping with a knife
Crying all night
Don't end your life

Stop!
Don't think about dying
When I ask if you're OK
It's hard to hear you crying

Stop!
Don't think you're a waste of space
Show them who the big boss is:
Stand tall and proud
And act like you don't give a toss.

Dibora Hadish (13)
King Solomon International Business School, Birmingham

Martin Luther King Jr

We remember Martin Luther King Jr,
He is honoured and too special even to this day
'I have a dream'
United together in this land that we strive
To find a way
That we live and unite together.

He wanted each of us to see
The beauty of equality.

He taught me the right way of life
Weak turn to strong
Lovingness instead of hatred.

His message was to set us free
Let his legacy continue

As we remember Martin.

Ashan Mills (13)
King Solomon International Business School, Birmingham

Body Image

Every day, I look into my mirror
It lies to me.

It tells me that I'm pretty, I'm skinny, I'm good enough
But I'm not.

It's all because I don't look like her:
The one in the magazine.
Maybe I should get an injection
To make me prettier and thinner?

I don't think that there is hope
For me to get on the track.
For society
Maybe this is the end of my popularity
And my sanity.

Lauren Edmeade (13)
King Solomon International Business School, Birmingham

Life After Death

What if there was a light at the end of the tunnel
But not the one you imagined?
What if that light was a beam to another hospital room?
Rebirth into another family
Another time
Country
Lifetime?

As time moves forward
You focus on the life you have now.

You begin to adapt to your surroundings
Hours, days, years
Forgetting your past life
Little traces return
Sound familiar
Déjà vu.

Aneika Cooper (13)
King Solomon International Business School, Birmingham

This Morning

God
This morning
Called your name. I really
Loved you in life.
In death, I'll do the same.

I wish I didn't
Cry
The way I did
Today
I was thinking of you and so many words
I didn't get
To say.

When tomorrow starts,
I'll think about us
Not being apart

I'll think about you being always in my heart.

Ludan Alawad (13)
King Solomon International Business School, Birmingham

My Family

Family is fantastic
From the day you were born, they have always
Been there
They're cuddly like a teddy bear.

They care for you
They buy you lots of shoes
And when you cry, they say
'Don't worry, boohoo.'

But sometimes, they don't cook you nice food
But hey, that's all I have to say for the day.

Zaynah Begum (13)
King Solomon International Business School, Birmingham

In The Name Of Manchester!

Manchester, Manchester,
What can we say about Manchester?
Busy streets, famous shops, children smiling with delight,
But all of that changed in just one night.

A man, from a different country, different religion,
With different-coloured skin,
Made a dreadful decision, which changed lives,
Chatting with the sharks, planning, planning,
But what?

Night comes, day ends, just like the story of people's lives,
Children are ready to spend time
With family and best mates,
Thinking of entering,
Ready for the fun that's ahead of them.

In the background, there he is,
His decision is made,
He steps forward, heart racing, but proud of his ways,
He's not thinking or believing that his decision is wrong,
But one minute he is gone.

Bang! Everything gone, the world forgotten,
But him remembered,
Everyone running and screaming and believing
That this is just a mistake

But no, they hear the words 'bomb' and 'terrorist'
And all hell breaks loose.

An hour later, hospitals swarmed with people,
But minds are consumed with worry,
Where is my child, what have they done,
What have they done?

Parents are told what has happened
And the tears turn into fire,
It's wrong, what did they do?
This is what the parents ask,
But no, police are still investigating
With no answers from the devastation.

The suicide bomb is found,
The devil inside,
Faces are dropped and so is the bomb.

Heaven opens but Hell is only open for one person
And only one person.
The terrorist, the terrorist, the terrorist,
That's who it is, the terrorist.

Bang! Everything gone, the world forgotten,
But him remembered,
Everyone running and screaming
And believing that it's just a mistake,
But no, they hear the words 'bomb'
And 'terrorist' and all hell breaks loose.

Caitlin Millington (13)
Litcham School, Litcham

Trapped

I don't belong here.
They talk to me as if I'm a three-year-old,
Constantly needing help and attention.
I was fine by myself, perfectly capable.
I shouldn't be here, not yet.
I'm not like the others;
My mind is still as sharp as it was fifty years ago.

My body won't move like it did in time gone by -
Stiff hands and feet make everyday tasks closer
To impossible day by day.
Simple things like doing a button
Or drinking from a glass takes great determination.
I'm a young soul trapped in an old body.
Outside my tiny room, people pass through the streets,
Busy with things to do, places to go,
People to see; the hubbub of life just out of my reach.
The view from my window is never different,
Only for the change of seasons that come and go.
The tree I see every day has more freedom than me,
Swaying as it pleases, waving at me, mocking me.

What I long for is taken for granted
By those that complain about the weather,
Their work or their chores.
What I would give to sit on a park bench with ease
And watch the world from a different view.

Days merge like grey watercolours,
Visitors come in frequently, but only stay
To make themselves feel better,
To lesson their guilt.

I miss my wife and long to be with her.
She is resting now, but I am still in torment.
Despite the horrors of the war,
A part of me longs to be back,
Moving, having friends, feeling like I belong,
And feeling like I have a purpose.

I've lost it all now.
What I wish for is not in this life.
Is this life worth living any more?

Liberty Blackmore (13)
Litcham School, Litcham

Refuge
(Dedicated to refugees everywhere)

The windless night
The dark abyss
The harrowing sights

The men who came
Eyes glinting like gleeful cats
The flames that burned
The people that crumpled
Like leaves on our trees

The face of Father
So cold and broken

The screams of Sister
So mournful and true

The running
The running

Me and Mother
Running, running

The checkpoint
The guards
The prodding
The poking

The running
The running

The boat
The boat
The promise
The false promise

The sea
The sea
The cold
The cold

Mother
So silent
So silent

The boat
The boat
Sinking
Sinking

The drowning
The drowning

The ship
The ship
The hands lifting me

The language
The language
So strange and new

The port
The station
Shouting
Crying
Swearing
The questions
I couldn't answer

My language
My language
The questions
The answers

The hands
The tears
The soothing

The phrase
'Come with me'

The running
The running
No more.

Felix Platt (12)
Litcham School, Litcham

Hidden

Darkness is a thing that everyone feels
Sometimes it just feels so surreal
Someone please help, it's not as easy as it seems
The constant feeling of being so alone
And trying to express it in a poem
And everybody acts like they hardly know them
Just because they think he's nutty in the head
But maybe if he had somebody that was always there
Maybe he wouldn't have to keep those thoughts hidden
And wouldn't have to care
People wonder why they don't see the signs
When everybody's hiding behind a mask
Behind their own design
Pain isn't just a thing inside
It's hidden on their skin as little scars
And everyone wonders why life is so bizarre
But as people grow more distant life fades like a care
Burning into ashes
As their entire mental health crashes
This is a big issue in the society of today
So process how some act when you ask them if they're OK?

Conner Curson (15)
Litcham School, Litcham

Pretty Pathetic Hate

Racism, sexism and discrimination,
These are all wrong, right?
But there are other problems that keep us up at night.
Homophobia, transphobia and misunderstanding,
Have reached a crash-landing.
Rejected, hurt and abandoned,
By many a religion, that has shunned,
Who claim to be loving,
Yet when we come for help and care
None of that do they share.

We're told 'you're not a boy'
As to them, we're just an emotion toy.
We're told 'pansexual and bisexual don't exist'
yet the problems with them I could list.
But I do not feel to shun them,
As they have done to me
And the truth they have to see.

Don't forget the others,
Who are ripped and hurt and torn,
Equality for all,
Is what we don't want to fall,
Thunder that falls, thunder that calls,
Lightning that glows
And even the sun that shines bright,
Will never show us 'the light'.

Do us all a favour,
And understand what I saw
From you last night,
Is a reason for us to keep up the fight.

Ada Everett (13)
Litcham School, Litcham

Fogitis

A winding body, a twisted tail,
Clawing arms, stretching limbs,
Contorted face, gnarled fingers,
Extending, unfolding, reaching.
Prowling in, slinking out,
Creeping low, gliding through
Across streets and alleys it moves.

Across Regents Park, over the Thames,
Moving onwards, no winds blow,
Pressed against windows, curled under doors,
Seeking, searching, sensing,
Blocking sunlight, bringing dusk,
Traffic muffled, beggars silenced,
Gangsters pass by, delaying violence.

A guiding purpose, a malign intent,
Forever onwards, task incomplete,
Hunting relentlessly, scouting around,
Probing, peeking, finding.
Drifting this way, tumbling that,
Forcing hope away and faith to recede,
It's getting thicker, harder to breathe.

It takes a breath, lets out a sinister hiss,
An echoing sound, eerie and quiet,
One many are unable to hear,
Growling, howling, snarling.

Sparkling droplets quickly appear
As it gets denser, covering the eyes,
Shrouding London in secrets and lies.

Georgina Denney (13)
Litcham School, Litcham

Words Of Mine

Like weapons falling from a mouth,
Striking a blow against a metal world,
Awaking our minds with starlit skies and passion.
Oh how we crave those sweeping words,
Etched across a page.

Framed against a blue sky,
Gracefully they dive, swallows.
Stumbling, we seek words.
Wishing to be wrapped in their cloak of wonder.

Eyes blind, I surround,
Greed outstretched with a welcoming hand.
Eager to taste those luscious captives.
Our cages far too small,
To contain those beating wings.
We sob, trapped in those halcyon days.
With glee dancing in their eyes, those words escape.

Yet they return to our gasping lips,
Feverishly I drink.

I whisper, my treasures far and wide.
Not knowing where they go, or what they seek.
Wondering if my aim is true,
Revelling for I know that those words,
Like dreams falling from my mouth,
Are words of mine.

Amelia Platt (15)
Litcham School, Litcham

Not Popular

I'm not alone, not unpopular,
I have friends I think,
They're here for me, just getting a drink,
Stop calling me unpopular,
Leave me alone,
Leave me be, let me go.

I'm alone, with nowhere to go,
I've got no friends, my house ain't a home,
I got one place to stay but... nowhere to go,
Been quiet too long, forgot how to talk,
Don't wanna be popular, terrifies me,
But just a little friendship would satisfy me.

I have no purpose here, should I die?
Cos no one ever stops to say 'hi',
Why is it me?
Give me some love please.

No, it's not me,
It's you, it's always you,
Neglecting and rejecting me,
No matter what point of view,
No matter who you are,
No matter which way you look at it,
It's your guy's fault,
I am not popular.

Charles Crook (13)
Litcham School, Litcham

Through Pain And Paper

Have you ever wondered,
If whatever hold you dearest,
Dropped you,
Fought you,
Broke you?
Whatever you dare to try
It's do or die,
It's time to bust out of cage,
Untie your rage,
Forget the cane,
Forget the pain.

It's time to tackle this trek,
Through the rain, as an emotional wreck,
I ain't got time on my side,
I need to go through this thing like a slide,
Like the tide,
This ride to stardom,
Seems at its farthest,
But I can see the light,
Work for it like a fight,
Intensity at its peak,
Pen to paper,
Write your thoughts,
Write without restrain

Give it all up,
For the dream,
Looks through the seams,
You'll make it.

And when you're on top
Remember what you fought through,
Remember your roots
No matter what.

Jack Raby (13)
Litcham School, Litcham

The Unknown Soldier

12th of March, 1916,
I am the unknown soldier,
From the unknown location,
Signed up at 17,
A journey for me,
I feel so free.

15th of May,
Us brothers in arms,
Marching through France,
Feeling the breeze,
Lovely green trees.

1st of July,
Walking on land so hot and dry,
Trying to dig trenches, I feel so weak,
I wish I could sleep.

20th of September,
My head feels light,
I couldn't sleep last night,
My mother's letter,
Made me feel better.

10th of November,
Artillery will render,
Wet feet, wet clothes in trenches so cold

Rats running by,
I fear I may die.

I am the unknown soldier,
Buried in Westminster Abbey,
Royal flowers adorn my grave,
Remember me for I was brave,
I am the unknown soldier.

Bayley Able (13)
Litcham School, Litcham

Syrian Crisis

Ambush after ambush,
Minute after minute.
Bullets fly by
And explosions in the distance,
Make your hairs prick up.

People scramble away,
By boat or by foot.
If the water is their choice,
Make it, they will not,
As the boats aren't good enough.

It only worsens,
Never getting better.
Kids are crying in the streets,
Men are crying, feeling weak,
Women are crying as they aren't allowed to speak.

You may say they deserve it,
But deserve it they do not,
There are innocent people,
Walking in the streets,
When you hear the pop, you know they'll drop.

Try to make it stop,
You cannot.

However, if you think they can pull through,
Try especially hard, they do,
But sometimes I wonder if it is all true.

Caleb Bower (13)
Litcham School, Litcham

The Social Media Ship

A colossal wave crashed into the vessel,
The vessel sighed but carried on its voyage,
Waves surrounded the ship, causing it to go off track.
The wave was not blue, it was white yet clear,
Resulting in confusion and madness,
The ship carried on sailing
Through the blindness the wave had brought.
They couldn't go any further, however much they fought.

The waves were becoming too much to handle,
Each breath of air was getting shorter,
Waves flooded onto the vessel
Making it hard to see and breathe,
The ship didn't give up,
It couldn't, it was being relied upon,
everyone was working hard, especially the crew,
However, nobody knew if this was actually true.

Can somebody tell me
Where is the love?

Alysha Jolie West (13)
Litcham School, Litcham

Changing Climate

Ice caps are melting
Because of us
Polar bears are dying
Yet people still allow it
As they betray their intellects.

The grass is ever browning
In China, where coal is used every day
Blocking the Earth's atmosphere
It kills us and wildlife
Yet people still deny it.

The government will take action
Yet people still deny it
Reverse the action they have taken
Creating nothing but trouble
Betraying their intellects.

So I say to people
Don't deny the truth
You betray your knowledge
Make a stand on the danger
Make your mark in the wall of society.

The world will die
If we don't change our mind
Don't deny
If you don't want to die!

Dominic Hancock (13)
Litcham School, Litcham

A Social Image

A social image, the typical girl
The perfect person in an imperfect world,
Women, judged, put down and wrecked,
No more gentlemen, just disrespect,
Flawless figure, who are you to dictate?
The world, overflowing with negativity and hate,
Those Facebook comments, barbaric, not just humour?
Stop, just think, suicide begins with one rumour.

They say it's fine, just a one off,
Except, it keeps happening, it doesn't stop
Until you sink into a world of sadness,
Can't get out,
My friends begin to worry and doubt,
It's too late, I have to go,
I constantly feel on an all time low,
Lights out; I'm done,
Congratulations social media, you've won.

Sian Freestone (13)
Litcham School, Litcham

Bad Weather

Blazing down upon life,
Ice caps vanishing day and night.
Once a tranquil Monday,
Now a painful Sunday.

Orange trees bright and shining,
Falling briskly more death by daylight.
Once-green leaves on trees,
Now orange falling towards the bees.

Surrounded by a blanket,
Comforting at times.
Otherwise deadly and untouchable,
Deadly even as a tiny ball.

The best weather, British?
Pouring of rain is typical.
Now the sun glares brightly,
Not going down quietly.

Global warming isn't a myth,
It's really whether you believe or not.
Climate change is real,
And it is a big deal.

Isaac Bower (13)
Litcham School, Litcham

Society

Welcome to society,
We hope you enjoy your stay,
You're told it's okay to love yourself,
But not too much, okay?

Make sure to be your own person,
And don't worry about what you wear,
However, don't stand out too much,
In fact, change the colour of your hair.

They say the world is your oyster,
You're allowed to be whatever you dream,
But you must achieve high grades and be confident
Or else you'll remain unseen.

The best part about this place,
The ultimate scary truth,
You live in a world where everyone blames society,
But society is made by you.

Sophia Louise Djiakouris (13)
Litcham School, Litcham

Cancer

Fighting for life and a cure,
Its ambition is to engulf its prey,
Unnoticed until it arrives,
Cancer is a big killer,
And it's not nice.

Its victims are innocent,
But what does it care?
It inflicts chaos and disturbing fear,
Witchcraft, like a fog,
Covering us all but taking only some.

It blinds and confuses,
I'm not a victim,
But I know someone who was,
It's a heartless killer,
But what does it care?

To fall into its trap,
Is a dangerous one,
A small and tiny pit,
It is not,
Cancer, you thoughtless killer!

Simon (12)
Litcham School, Litcham

Pray, Please Pray For Manchester

A week ago
When light ran low
The media played a ballad
A sorrow song
For 22 gone
And 59 lay wounded
So pray, please pray for Manchester

In Greater Manchester
Times have been better
But today the people lay still
For those attacked
And those who lay innocent
It's time to say goodbye
So, pray, please pray for Manchester

Whatever provoked them?
Whatever we said?
What did we do to deserve this?
What you think's right
Has done much wrong
Many we love have gone
So pray, please pray for Manchester.

Danielle Mia Harrowing (13)
Litcham School, Litcham

Terrorism

Terrorists terrorise,
Hypnotised puppet,
Burning the religious rubber,
Bombing the innocent,
Suicide bombers locked up in denial.
It's like a disease created to please
The Devil's own tease.
Terror is their weapon,
They pray for fear mongers,
Burning with hate.
Is your god a coward?
Whom you do believe.
Is he a numb and dumb idol?
Fools you in your sleep.
One thing left is stand,
Not to respond with fear,
To the wicked terror,
We, who are not afraid
Shall take back the power
And break those terrorising.

Ben Wilson (12)
Litcham School, Litcham

The Aspects Of The Mind

Believe,
Tomorrow you may leave.
To see,
Something you need.
Come on,
You could be gone,
But no.

Hope,
That's good but nope.
It's false.
Not even a little true.
It's a lie,
That makes you cry,
Use a tissue.

Inspire,
Do not hire.
Stay here,
It's better up than down.
Don't be alone,
You have a home,
Live.
Create,
Don't hate.

Keep them,
The art of yourself.
It's not over,
There's more to cover,
Be yourself.

Sophie Adelaide Stangroom (13)
Litcham School, Litcham

North Korea

Imagine a life with no equal rights,
Where woman are raped,
And where there's no lights,
No way to escape.

No music in the background,
Only one channel on TV,
No one to make a sound,
No way to escape.

Where you're told how to dress,
And how to do your hair,
Your life, a mess,
No way to escape.

You may watch your parents' death,
But you're not allowed to cry,
When you witness their last breath,
No way to escape.

Ella Westhorpe (13)
Litcham School, Litcham

Life

Trees falling,
How appalling.
Animals dying,
Even if we're trying.
People go missing every day,
Will they come back today?
Life is a sad place,
Things disappear without a trace.

Life is like a roller coaster
Going up,
But always coming down.

So even if you aren't feeling bold,
You never know what tomorrow will hold.
So don't be sad,
And always be glad,
Even if life brings you down,
Try and get up without a frown.

Evelyn Scott (13)
Litcham School, Litcham

That's Reality

Gorgeous girls,
Beautiful boys,
Every comment with wide heart eyes.
What about me?
What about you?
With us, it's all just lies.

Stunning selfies,
Hashtag fit,
A like for every post of theirs.
What about me?
What about you?
With us, nobody really cares.

Ugly smiles,
Shameful bodies,
A tear every time the camera clicks.
What about me?
What about you?
With us, this is reality.

Scarlett Stevens (13)
Litcham School, Litcham

Combined Society

I'm lying in a king-sized bed,
You're lying on the floor.
I live in a house,
You live outside the mall.
I have the newest iPhone,
You have the Nokia brick.
I can pay for Michelin star,
You can't pay for chips.
I leave my windows open daily,
You, however, have no door.
My life is full of love,
Your heart is always sore.
I walk past you, beggar,
You look up in awe.
I am rich
And, you are poor.

Millie Fisher (13)
Litcham School, Litcham

Love?

What is love?
Is it something from above?
Why does it hurt?
It makes me feel like I'm dirt.

Am I worth it?
It's like a hit
I hate crying
I always presume you're lying.

Do I matter
Or am I like a Mad Hatter?
Very confused
Mentally abused.

What's the point?
I just disappoint
I want to die.

Amber Hayden (12)
Litcham School, Litcham

Animals

Some are big,
Some are small,
Some are tall,
Some are short.

Some have long necks,
Some have short legs,
Some have long tails,
Some have short ears.

Some are cheeky,
Some are nice,
Some are beautiful,
Some are hairy.

But some have no brains at all,
That is what animals are like.

Jessica Elizabeth Edwards (12)
Litcham School, Litcham

The Hernia

I was only a wee little lad
When I got my first surgery.
In the hospital bed I lay,
Chillin' with me mum.
Off I went into surgery
Some drugs had knocked me out cold.

Waking up, I was as high as the stars
Off I was to the universe
All there was, was me and the planets
With some flying granite.

Danny Benson (13)
Litcham School, Litcham

Gone Mad

Started off as an MC,
But maybe I should have been an MP instead,
Because none of these guys make sense, noooo.

It's like I'm living in backward times,
Nobody's on job,
They're all just sitting around
Arguing about bombs.

I hate how the world's like this.

Levi List (13)
Litcham School, Litcham

Equality

Do you ever wonder,
What goes through people's heads
When they say...

Comments,
That tear people apart,
Get them down,
Turn their world upside down.

So please be careful about what you say,
And tomorrow's world
Will be better than today's.

Katie Duthie (13)
Litcham School, Litcham

22nd

Start of a new year,
A beginning to a new chapter of life,
But soon it will bring a tear,
As the clouds start to darken,
A threat so hard to fight,
Tragic incidents to take place,
Horrific acts bring cities together,
Bringing the light from dark,
Making us stand strong forever.

Megan Day (14)
Litcham School, Litcham

A Girl's Best Friend

Four big proud paws ready to pounce,
Coat so smooth it can't help but bounce,
Ears like a chamois leather,
Nose as rough as the surface of the moon,
Two twinkling eyes like stars showing endless love,
My buddy, my best friend!

Boe Wilcox (13)
Litcham School, Litcham

Rainbow

The rainbow is colourful, calm and free
Will there be treasure waiting for me?
It glows so bright in the light,
Will there be a tide tonight?
Birds singing all night,
Would there be any sleep tonight?

Caitlin Hawkins
Litcham School, Litcham

Stuck

I'm breaking
I can't be fixed
I'm missing
But I won't be missed.

Still shaking
From what I fear.
I can't let you in
So don't come near.

I guess you're right
I'm way too thin,
And I'm fighting a battle
That I'll never win.

I have so many flaws
I don't know where to start.
From my messed-up hair
To my messed-up heart.

So what's the point
To continue to fight?
When my restless days
Turn into restless nights.

This life hasn't been fair
I can finally tell,
And it hurts like hell.

I still don't understand,
What was God's cause?
Why did He put me on Earth
With all my flaws?

Was I just born to die?
Am I part of a plan?
Made to finally see
That I won't die an old man.

I don't know how to live,
I have nothing to gain,
And all I want from you
Is to end all my pain.

I'm losing sight
Of what I've already seen.
I'm losing my grip
And I'm barely seventeen.

Artin Shey (15)
Meole Brace School Science College, Shrewsbury

Signed Your Name

Get dressed, love.
You're going to be late.
You look at yourself in the mirror.

Put it down, love.
It's caused you so much pain.
You're going to do damage.
You don't want to be called insane.

Stand up, love.
Your tears make you weak.
Wipe off that black mascara.
Proof of sadness upon your cheek.

Take your pills, love.
You must try your best.
Forget about your dizzy spells,
The tightening in your chest.

Chin up, love.
No one can know your thoughts.
You must act like you're happy
While your heart just sits and rots.

Smile a little, love.
Let me see those pearly whites.
No one has to know
What you thought about all those nights.

Breathe for me, love.
Your pain won't be forever.
Take my hand, and I'll take yours.
We'll get through this together.

Jade Hamilton (13)
Meole Brace School Science College, Shrewsbury

I Won't Be Missed

I have so many fears
I don't know where to start
So what's the point
I won't be missed.

Still shaking
From what I fear
I'm losing the battle
But I won't be missed.

I have so many flaws
I don't know where to start
From my fat thighs
To my messed-up life.

So what's the point
To continue this pain
When my long days
Turn to long nights.

This life is painful
Full of pain
Why carry on
When it hurts like hell?

I don't know how to live
I don't know why I should live
I have nothing to gain
I'm losing grip.

I've lost the battle
It's over
The pain will be ended
But I won't be missed.

Chloe Marie Unwin
Meole Brace School Science College, Shrewsbury

You Don't Know Her

Do you wanna know her?
Do you wanna try?
Her life's a little complicated
Let me tell you why.
She feels unloved, unwanted
She cries six times a day
Her heart is nearly broken
She's in a lot of pain
She cuts herself to feel
That's how she plays her games
She smiles at the blade
Like blood is summer rain.

Do you still wanna know her?
Do you still wanna try?
Do you think her life is complicated?
Too late, that girl died
She screamed and cried for help
Hoped for a way out
She was trapped in a world of hate
A world of lies and tears
She lay on her bed at night
And wondered, *Why am I still here?*
And when she fell asleep
Nightmares haunted her dreams.

Jade Chloe Cox (15)
Meole Brace School Science College, Shrewsbury

This Is The Life Of The Theatre Unseen

You arrive, it's time,
You are shaking inside,
This is the life of the theatre unseen.

The swish of a dress,
The clip-clop of your shoes,
This is the life of the theatre unseen.

The spray of perfume,
The touch of make-up,
This is the life of the theatre unseen.

A lost shoe,
A ripped dress,
This is the life of the theatre unseen.

The squeals of excitement,
The tears of nerves,
This is the life of the theatre unseen.

The blackness of the audience,
The blinding lights on you,
This is the life of the theatre unseen.

A perfect performance,
A stress-free time,
This is the life of the theatre seen.

Ciara Lucas-Garner (12)
Meole Brace School Science College, Shrewsbury

The Common Killer

Depression is a killer.
It takes many lives
Who could have it next?
Your sister and your wife?
I used to believe depression wasn't real,
Just a figure of speech used by adults about how they feel.
But then, it hit me like a truck.
Depression is real and if you have it life can suck.

If you have depression there is always someone there.
Someone to get you through life and this nightmare.

Robbie Richards (13)
Meole Brace School Science College, Shrewsbury

Everyone's Unique

It's not anyone's fault
Just because they're different
It's not anyone's fault
Don't knock their confidence
Please don't make fun of them
It won't just hurt them
It'll hurt their family, including their mum
It's not anyone's fault
Just because they're different
It's not anyone's fault
Don't knock their confidence.

Matthew James Cumming (13)
Meole Brace School Science College, Shrewsbury

Life Can Be Hard

Life can be hard,
When you feel like everything is against you,
Doesn't matter what you try and do,
It doesn't go to plan.

Life is so hard,
What have I done wrong?
Feelings engulf me,
Leaving me sad and lonely.

I wish I could feel happy again
But I don't know how to,
Life can be hard.

Owen Sadd (13)
Meole Brace School Science College, Shrewsbury

Trapped

They don't know what it's like,
They don't know how it feels,
All these eyes looking by,
Everything still, time on standby.

Even though they aren't looking straight.
Feeling like no one is your mate.
But no one listens
But you have to pretend.

James Adcock (15)
Meole Brace School Science College, Shrewsbury

Hidden Meanings - Haiku

Brittle temptation
Cracked to a thousand pieces
But there is no life.

Aidan Blake (14)
Meole Brace School Science College, Shrewsbury

My World

She smiles, my world stops
Reality ends and fantasy begins
Then bruises due to walls of love.
Love hurts.
Fantasy goes, reality hits
She is like the sun:
She's bright.
She brings it all.
The world sharpens,
It focuses on her

My heart beats wildly like a drum
She makes me a better person
She lifts my confidence
I am whole when she talks to me.

Ethan Mark Provis (12)
Ormiston Denes Academy, Lowestoft

Untitled

Rhino,
Majestic, massive,
Killed for their horns,
The feature that gives their character,
3 days is all it takes,
For 50 rhinos to die,
The dark's the time,
For rhinos this is deadly.

Ivory trade's illegal,
Don't do it, it's wrong,
We need to stop the poachers,
Or in 15 years rhinos will be gone.

Abigail Crame (12)
Ormiston Denes Academy, Lowestoft

Silent Company

Company.
Unjudging company.
He keeps the secrets that no human can keep,
He is my security.

He has a heart and soul,
His soulful eyes capture me,
His silence means I can be free in life,
Without fear or anxiety.

Company.
Eternal loving company.
He is my one and only,
He is my comfort bear...

George Richard Eric Sibbald (11)
Ormiston Denes Academy, Lowestoft

A Normal Day?

A normal day.
She got sick
They tried to mute me but
I had to know what
Was happening.
A tumour.
A choice:
To suffer or sleep forever.
I whispered my goodbye
The tears fell; grief unending.
Devastation.

Kelsey Earp (11)
Ormiston Denes Academy, Lowestoft

Difference

Jainie has big lips and Lainie has a slim figure.
Jade has a tight jawbone, that is not natural.
They can't handle the fact of being fat
Or to have big cheeks.
They cannot handle the fact that natural is even an option.
They have to listen.
These girls are no longer pretty
Or good-looking or even have a nice personality,
Just because they can't reach for the stars
Or because they can't feel connected.
Just because Sarah has high heels that support her.
You can't be supported,
Just because Jennifer has lipstick,
You can't match her.
If you can't be yourself, why bother?
We bother to be ourselves
To make an appearance.
We focus more on subtraction than attraction.
We know who we are
And what we are,
So let's just be ourselves.

Jea Franks (12)
Pakefield High School, Lowestoft

Whale's Story

A whale,
With a flappy tail,
Who just likes to sail,
And deliver mail.
One day he discovers a jail,
But a shark finds the whale's trail.
When the whale sees the shark,
He stabs him with a nail
But then the whale fails
Then the shark bites his tail,
And puts him in jail.
His trail was a very good fail!
All of a sudden it starts to hail,
And the lucky whale gets out of jail!
When he's out he meets another whale called Gail
Who is female,
And he falls in love with that whale,
Then they get a pet sea snail!

The shark is back,
Out to attack,
With his friend, Jack,
Who is able to track.
They go on a train called Blu-Tac,
Then they meet another shark called Nic Nak,
Then they found the enemy's track
And found them in a shack!

The family of whales,
Oh and don't forget the snail,
They are all back in jail,
The problem is that you can only eat kale,
In jail!

Leanne (11), Ellie Beenham, Evie & Rosie Elizabeth Graham
Pakefield High School, Lowestoft

Let Me Be Me

I'm here to talk about equality
Because, quite simply, it seems to me
That you don't want to live peacefully
And I'm not gonna let it go easily.

I've seen you use 'gay' insultingly
And some people, you know, they're just meant to be,
It doesn't matter 'bout sexuality
You know love just comes naturally.

You need to change your ways dramatically
And yeah, I know you disagree
And I'm sorry that we think differently
But please, can you just let me be me?

Rachel Louise Sewell (13)
Pakefield High School, Lowestoft

Untitled

Why does our appearance affect our education?
'Pull your skirt down!'
'Roll down your sleeves!'
'Take off your make-up!'
Why, so I can learn better?
'Tuck your shirt in!'
'Only black shoes!'
'Top button up!'
What, will it teach me to read?
Students should be able to express themselves!
They should be able to feel confident!
Students should show their talents!
Why should I?
Why, so I can learn better?
Why does our appearance affect our education?

Chloe Rose Jacobs (12)
Pakefield High School, Lowestoft

Image

We are not perfect!
We are not made to be perfect!
Stop, stop portraying girls as 'perfect'
Perfect, perfect, perfect.

Perfect skin,
Perfect hair,
Perfect bodies everywhere.

Why?
Why ruin girls?
Why, just why?

Why filters?
Why Photoshop?
Why airbrush?

You're saying we need to look at these airbrushed models
But no!

We are not made to be perfect,
So stop,
Or humanity will be dead!

Tabitha Bond (13)
Pakefield High School, Lowestoft

Image

The way you look shouldn't matter
Whether you're black, white, big, small or thin
Don't judge a person by their outside
Because what's on the inside is what matters.

The way you look shouldn't matter
Don't judge a person by their image
Because through everything that happens
Judging people can cause damage.

When you use the knife
It can really change someone's life.

Kelsey Leech (13)
Pakefield High School, Lowestoft

Identity

Trying to hide our identity
Cos you don't want it to effect you mentally,
Hiding in make-up.
Never wanting to wake up to society,
Getting told to show who you really are,
Afraid to say, afraid to show,
What you really are,
Hiding from the truth.
Wanting to go back to when you were you,
Being judged from when you wake.
Making you shiver and shake.
Thinking you're just a mistake.

Amelia Gow (12)
Pakefield High School, Lowestoft

Identity

Why should people be anxious about what others think.
Putting loads of make-up on, then still feeling queer.
Eating all the green food that doesn't fill your stomach.
Having the right figure that will impress all the others.
Being pretty is hard work but society sets the standards.
What beauty do we have if we have none on the inside?

Molly Bullard (13)
Pakefield High School, Lowestoft

Just People

Racism racing rapidly like rabbits
But racism shouldn't be racing
It should be squished like ants under your feet
Being bulldozed with a bulldozer
We are all equal
Black, white, Asian, mixed, African
We are all equal
Caribbean, Japanese, all of us equal
We are all just people!

Trinity Meadez (13)
Pakefield High School, Lowestoft

Society Smile

Everyone is so caught up in what they are doing,
They don't realise they are moving,
Moving someone else's mood meter,
Moving it to the unhappy side,
Think...
Link up and do something to change that meter,
Don't be so caught up,
It doesn't take much to just, just smile.

Jack James Jefferies (13)
Pakefield High School, Lowestoft

Untitled

Putting an image on someone can change their life,
It can feel like someone has stabbed you in the back
With a knife,
Calling someone fat or thin,
Ugly or dumb
Can change someone.
So don't point out people's issues
Because they could cry and need lots of tissues.

Amber Hill (13)
Pakefield High School, Lowestoft

Bullying

You never know what someone is going to say,
So don't call them annoying, lonely or gay.
People say that they are okay,
But really, are they?
You don't know what is going on in someone's life,
So don't make them use a knife.

Xander Dennis (13)
Pakefield High School, Lowestoft

When I'm Older

Sometimes life can be a little hard,
But I'm going to save the day and be a junior life guard.
When I'm older I'm going to have a fit wife and two kids,
And two pucker cars and a good life.
What will fall out of my pockets is a 50 pound note,
I can swim like a fish, I can even float.
When it comes to life saving, I'm the potion.
I can save people from the sea
And even the Pacific Ocean.
When it comes to fighting, it isn't a joke.
I can swim forward, even back stroke.
I survive in a current and I'll dive if I have to
'Cause I'm the man they'll go to.

Bradley Garratt (13)
Sandwell Community School - Wednesbury Campus, Hydes Road

Life Rap

Sometimes in life I'm a bit of a joker
I laugh with the drinkers, laugh with the smokers.
I'm the one who has loads of laughs,
I'm ten times more exciting than maths.
I'm a comic, watch me on the stage,
My jokes are so live, they jump off the page.

Sometimes the girls think I'm fit and funny,
I think the girls are as sweet as honey.
One thing a girl likes is a little bit of humour,
That's a fact, guys. It's not a rumour.

Cameron Martin (13)
Sandwell Community School - Wednesbury Campus, Hydes Road

Life Rap

I want to treat people with love, respect and honour,
You can always communicate with the Connor.
And there's no one out there who's sharper.
So remember the name. Harper.

Connor Harper (12)
Sandwell Community School - Wednesbury Campus, Hydes Road

Bad Changes

Tears in my eyes, I'm about to cry.
I get down on my knees, but get no reply.

'Why?' I say, as I realise my life is about to change.
Dad isn't here any more; it feels empty and strange.

'Everyone gets used to it' except for me.
It feels like there's a hole, a space in our family tree.

I want to let it out, stop keeping it inside.
It feels like my whole life has been a rollercoaster ride.

New house, new people, new lifestyle.
Everything is different but I will get used to it after a while.

Suddenly, money is very precious to us.
We are going to the bankers; it will be discussed.

I feel angry, confused, frustrated at the same time.
When your parents divorce
It feels like they have committed a crime.

No one really understands unless it's happened to them too,
As it's hard to figure what they have been through.

Charlotte Upcott (11)
Seaford College, Petworth

Where Has All The Music Gone?

Music was one of the great things in life.
Freedom of expression and a place to forget your strife.
However, somewhere in the 90s, and I say this with dismay,
A dark cloud hovered over the music industry
That still lingers today.

Let's start with the singers if you can even call them that.
Attention junkies expecting fame at the drop of the hat.
Take a look at Bieber, a prime example of that,
A spoilt, rich, irritating brat.
His first song, the abomination called 'Baby'
Drove many an adolescent female crazy.
There is no real substance, don't even assume.
It's just repetitive lyrics and lots of autotune.
Now let's attack the lyrics which is what comes next.
Drinking, driving and especially sex.
Haven't you forgotten there are kids out there too?
What if they start thinking these are cool things to do?
Let's trace our minds back to the last generation
Where lots of the music back then was an inspiration.
Do you see singers like that today - no.
Partying yobbish druggies. The woe, the woe.

These atrocities against music are a crying shame
But the so-called singers, they are not to be blamed.
It's the marketing companies at whom we should be mad.
They're the reason why music today is ever so bad.

All these greedy managers, they find all this funny.
They're laughing at you and taking your money.
They exploit all these singers and then
They turn them into bank accounts for them.
It disgusts me that today this musical trash
Solely revolves around marketing and cash.

To illustrate the final point I'm about to make,
The junk in the charts is not real, it's just fake.
There are so many real singers
Who aren't getting the chance
Because of morons like these who can't sing or dance.
Nowadays you can pick up anyone on the street
So long as they have fit bodies and nice cheeks.
What's the point in looks and no talent to give?
If that's the way we're thinking, I'd sooner not live.
Throw that garbage out the window
And get some good taste.
There is more to music than just a pretty face.

Marcus Fairweather (14)
Seaford College, Petworth

The Bullied

Imagine, looking out into the world
Your eyes infrared, cameras sensing danger.
Imagine being scared of every corridor,
Corner, ceiling and floor
Terror coursing through your fast-flowing blood vessels.
Imagine a drum's sound
Reverberating throughout your body,
Your eyeballs almost shaking within your pulsating skull.

Your brain, a Jägerbomb of horrors
Intensified by the things they said,
The things they did.
Even a knife on the plate you eat off
Just a way to forget some words
That even your maths teacher may have said.

Fists thrusting forwards arrogantly and angrily,
Wind whistles as they cut through
As though it were just skin on the forearm.
Jawbone separating in two like torn paper.
Sounds like ice falls dropping off into an abyss.
Shamefully the sociopath attacking the poor broken soul
Doesn't even break a tear through their dark sullen face
When others would cry themselves to sleep
Curled in the foetal position.

Don't tell me 'no one cares' because, I care, I care!
So ignore them, distort them and contort them
But don't retort them they weren't,
Aren't and won't ever damn well be worth it,
They aren't human.
To the bullied... 'We do care.'

Toby Loeffen-Ames (14)
Seaford College, Petworth

I Have A Question?

Someone tell me what happened to the love?

That beautiful love that people used to have for the world.
That special love you have
For all our peers at an innocent five.
Why now do we suffocate our world?
With fumes and trash and oil and hate?
Why when we grow up do we start to judge our friends?
And hurt those we love?

Someone tell me what happened to the happiness?

That joyful feeling you get
Through your body when you're younger.
Those moments when you laugh so hard
Your stomach aches!
Why now do we need pills to make us happy?
Why now, instead of laughing,
Do we cry till our whole body aches?

Is that where the story ends?
Aren't we made for better?
Can we access more?

The joy of memories past.
The love in an encouraging word.
The unconditional affection when you return home.

There is unrivalled beauty in a glowing sunset.
And there is serenity in the last light of day.

Maybe the love never left?
Or maybe you gave the happiness away?
Could it be about something else?
Something more important?

Perhaps, sometimes we all just need,
To change where we look...

Ella Kuchanny (14)
Seaford College, Petworth

Stereotypes

I'm British born and bred,
I know what you're thinking,
Another tea sipping, crumpet fed,
Posh accent, top hat head.

If you insist on being like that,
This will be interesting but let's see,
I run fast, you assume I'm black?
Wrong, so I'm white, I must be racist.

I'm Christian and I can't walk on water,
And I don't believe in religious slaughter,
I study the Muslim religion,
But I don't fit the Muslim description.

I don't wear robes head to toe,
I ate a burger last night with a side of fries,
So I'm American through your eyes?
But I'm not fat and I don't speak like a cowboy.

My best friend was born in China,
And here we go again,
He doesn't eat dog or have yellow skin,
Nor does he have a straight A education.
So it's time to make up your mind,
Am I a posh Brit, a racist white
A Muslim, Christian begging for a fight?

Or am I a Yank or a dog-eating straight A student?

I'll let you decide...

Tom Jillians (14)
Seaford College, Petworth

You're Different

They say the clothes you wear are weird,
They say you have to wear make-up
Or you won't be revered.
You might not have clear skin but is that really a sin?
You are you,
And you are unique.
If everyone, everywhere looked the same,
This world would be boring and lame.
People are judged by the way they look,
And what they are interested in,
But from your point of view they are all alike.
Society and media has made people this way,
You are told what to wear and you have to be perfect,
But they are leading us astray.
If you're not in the popular group you are an outcast,
But is that really true?
People don't act themselves,
And they fit in with everyone else.
But is that really a good thing?
So don't waste your time
Trying to become something you're not,
Because being different is beautiful.
You are your truest self,
And you are unique!

Lottie Amy Hubbard (14)
Seaford College, Petworth

Fatherland

They were told to fight for the Fatherland.
They were told it would be over by Christmas.
They were told *Dulce et Decorum est.*
They were told they would change the nation.

They watched the demon's pantomime.
They watched the firing of the guns.
They watched the bombs drop.
They watched their comrades fall.

They heard the howling of men at night.
They heard the chatter of the rats.
They heard the sergeant say, 'The war will be over soon.'
They heard the Spitfires and Messerschmitts above.

They suffered the pain of Hell.
They suffered the pain of death.
They suffered the pain of war
And they prayed for the war to end.

Rafe Ernest Nisbet (12)
Seaford College, Petworth

People

People come in all shapes and sizes:

Some are tall, some are short
Everyone is different
People are skinny or port.

Humans can come in all sizes from fat to thin
Which I can understand, but I don't understand
Why they are judged by the colour of their skin.
It makes no sense because we are all the same inside.
Pink.
So why would you assume from the outside
About in what they confide?

Why would you assume someone's potential
Over just a single differential?

It is a discrimination of so many different populations.

So why
Why do it?

We're all the same!

Alfie Wakefield (14)
Seaford College, Petworth

This Is Real

OK, I'm a woman.
What's the big deal?
This is my life,
And this is real.

You tell me what I can and can't wear,
But answer me: how is this fair?
Just because I'm different,
Different to you,
Why do you tell me what I can and can't do?

Why are men treated differently to me?
Can you tell me why? Because I don't see.
Is it my eyes, or even my hair?
This is my life,
But it's not fair.

OK, I'm a woman,
What's the big deal?
This is my life,
And this is real.
This is my life,
But it's not fair.

Amy Styles (11)
Seaford College, Petworth

Parents

They nag me to go to bed at half six
And do not appreciate my cool tricks.
They make me do my terrible homework,
They hate it when I am trying to twerk.
They blame me when my pet dog eats Dad's shoes.
They think my boyfriend is just boring news.
They make me eat disgusting broccoli
And try to be cool very awkwardly.
But Mum gives me advice on what to wear
And Dad is my cuddly teddy bear.
Oh, I love Mum's special Sunday dinner.
They always make me feel like a winner.
When I grow up there will be a time when
I hope to be a parent just like them.

Charlotte Brinsmead (12)
Seaford College, Petworth

NHYS

Never hate yourself,
The way you speak,
The way you look,
The clothes you wear.
Everyone is different and the same.
You might have a banana-shaped smile
Or elephant ears,
Eyes like eggs.
You may have spots,
But it doesn't matter.
Maybe you are taller than all your friends,
But it doesn't matter.
Or maybe you have long or short hair for a boy or a girl.

Never hate yourself.
The way you speak,
The way you look,
Is you.
Your friends will never put you down.
Never hate yourself.

Tom Thornton (12)
Seaford College, Petworth

The State

Lots of people go to state school,
To be honest I feel for them,
The best of state schools are the worst,
Nobody deserves 'the state'.

Many people find school tough,
State schools only make it tougher,
The facilities are rough,
Nobody deserves 'The State'.

The facilities are bad,
So are all the staff,
None of them can teach that well,
Nobody deserves 'The State'.

Blocked-up toilets,
Cafeteria empty,
Shouting teachers,
Nobody deserves 'The State'.

Lewis Fox (14)
Seaford College, Petworth

The Mendacious Media

The media forms your opinion
So don't be a minion
Stand strong
You have done nothing wrong
They have control
So don't enrol
In their spurious drivel
Which will make you uncivil
It is the bait
Which will influence your decision on your fate
Therefore, it's easy not to see
What the media has come to be
So if you choose not to fight
You may lose your right
To the freedom of your life
Regardless of the strife
You should take effect
Never just rely on the media
But on your own intellect.

Tabitha Hill (14)
Seaford College, Petworth

Garden Life

Dancing fairies on a sun-swept lawn,
Swaying in the wind, going back and forth,
Smiling faces bathing in the sun,
Buzzy bees feast for fun.

Glistening dew in the early morning,
Eaten by snails, dark at night,
Growing again throughout the day.
Shooting leaves up into the sky.

Jack Frost comes and spoils the fun,
They begin to wither, their heads bow down.
The ice freezes their vulnerable bodies,
But the strength comes from underground.

They dream of happier days to come.

Molly Holt (12)
Seaford College, Petworth

Identity

Don't pretend to be someone you're not,
Be who you really are and you can have friends,
Don't be a stranger,
Be our friend,
Don't lie about who you are
When you've done something wrong,
Be the person who rips off the mask,
Don't be scared,
Be one of us,
Don't be the one who goes to the dark side,
Be the one whose light shines out,
Don't be the one who gets arrested for committing a crime,
Be the one who stops crime,
Your identity is a crime fighter.

Benjamin Cotton (12)
Seaford College, Petworth

Bully

Kicked in a corner on my hands and knees
People start staring and laughing at me.

My heart's in my stomach
While my hands and knees start to bleed.
What have I done to deserve this?
I think as they kick me.

I'm scared and deserted and I start to scream,
'Stop, stop, now stop picking on me.'

I pick up the courage and stand up and say,
'Just because I'm a bit different
Never gives you the right to bully me anyway.'

Lola Andrews (11)
Seaford College, Petworth

Confidence

You are who you are and you can't change,
There is no one else like you; you are unique!
In life people will try and pin you down,
Most of those people are insecure.
Your confidence makes you who you are,
Some people might say you're too confident
Or you're not confident enough.
Let them say it, you don't have to listen,
Only you can change who you are
But why change when everyone else is taken.
There's no one else like you - embrace it!

Daisy Bassett (14)
Seaford College, Petworth

Attention

I hate people trying to get attention
And they do it by intention
They make up lies
About their lives
And to never think how it could affect
The people they neglect
When they talk about their fancy lives
It brings tears to people's eyes
Who have less
Less than a girl with an expensive headdress
For the people that get caught up
I'm saying, don't give up
That's why I'm making a stand
Against the people, I cannot stand.

Henry McMorran (14)
Seaford College, Petworth

An Envy Man

Down the streets,
An envy man:
High shoulders,
Small feet.

Down the streets,
An envy man:
No hair,
Green eyes.

Down the streets,
An envy man:
Fingers like claws,
Rats at his heels.

Down the streets,
An envy man:
Scissors to hand,
Jewellery bulging out of his pockets.

Mandy Rabina (12)
Seaford College, Petworth

Words Are Tears

Words are tears,
Emotion flowing in rivulets,
Meaning drowning in streams,
Love trickling in droplets,
Happiness streaming in rivers,
Horror swimming in lakes.
Words are the tears of the world.

Abbie Biggs (12)
Seaford College, Petworth

Tyrants Of The World

Kingdoms rise and kingdoms fall,
They have throughout the years,
And while none have fallen for quite a while,
That has not quelled our fears.

People ravenous with power,
Have ripped apart society,
Some groups have even hidden,
Behind the powerful wall of piety.

Through political power or buildings bombed,
The delusional have found their way,
And while they were put down by 'good',
Others have still gone awry.

And while these people were taken out,
And relinquished from command,
From the Nazis to the Soviets,
And all who sprung alarms.

We stand on a new horizon,
The transition from the old world to the new,
Will we learn from our ancestors' mistakes,
Or will we obliterate this world of new?

Our future walks on a wobbly bridge,
Which can be shattered by the lightest touch,
And if that falls into the abyss,
I'll be able to say, 'I told you as much'.

Charly Peter Spurge (12)
St Clements High School, King's Lynn

The Swing

Swinging in a back and forwards motion,
Much like my emotions,
Happiness seems caged,
And I'm filled with rage,
I'll bite it and fight it,
But with no weapon to slice it,
I might try to drown all the pain,
Happiness surfaces until the pain has drunk the lake.
Looks on my face are mistakes,
And I pace for a thought,
That I can grab, take hold of.
Be normal again.
But my normality is locked in a pen,
I don't have a key,
I lost it to a friend,
To whom I did freely lend.
But who I lost trust in,
Just like my emotions,
My thoughts swing in a back and forwards motion.

Saying that I don't care wouldn't be fair,
I care a lot, I swear,
And I want to be happy for what we have,
Don't get me wrong, I'm glad,
But it seems forced,
And possessive rather than the love,
Humans once shared.

But now we're paired,
With people we don't like,
Because our friends give dares.
So we paint our faces with a smile,
The paint not waterproof,
Then it rains and pours for a while.
We're expected to be happy,
After all I'm just a child,
But it's impossible,
When your emotions swing,
In a back and forwards motion.
And they'll switch for a while,
So people will never be sure,
Whether I'm joyous or miserable,
And they'll have pity,
Or think I'm silly.
Busy cities remind me of a place,
Filled with many things,
But all so quiet, so calm.
Held by a steady palm.
And yet again have my emotions swung,
In a back and forwards motion.

All our emotions sit on swings,
And if you're weak,
You'll be stuck

If you're strong however,
You'll begin to swing rapidly,
For what seems forever,
Until you're strong enough to break the chain.
Your past doesn't have to define you.
Good or bad.
You don't have to be,
Permanently sad.
When you take control of your emotions,
They don't have to swing in a back and forwards motion.

Jasmine Elise Chapman (11)
St Clements High School, King's Lynn

Hate Truth?

My voice feels faded
My heart feels weak
Voice not heard
I'm scared
And alone
Tempted to scream
Cry for help
Lord have mercy
Why me?
Why me?
I know self-harming is not the way
But the way I feel
I cannot explain
Save me from my pain.

Madison Angel Rudd (11)
St Clements High School, King's Lynn

Me And Peter Pan

Me and Peter Pan playing in the sand
Watching the planes as they land
As we listen to the sky
We hear sweet birds tweeting as they fly.
Next, we go to the shops, hearing people saying,
'Hurry up, chop, chop!'
Mothers buying their children lollipops
Whizzing, buzzing, go the flies
Each one swooping and looping in the sky,
Others saying their merry goodbyes
The shop closes down for the night.
The 10th of July, Peter Pan's birthday is nearby
Just wait... all the months will whizz by
Like an angel in the sky
A couple of months pass by.
Today is the day
We celebrate this special day
It's Peter Pan's birthday.
He flies around the room saying,
'Cock-a-doodle-doo!'
He teaches me how to fly
So off we go into the night sky,
We never think negative
Because we're always positive...

Off we go into the sky
Because me and Peter Pan
We know how to fly.

Alex Ubakanma (13)
Stanground Academy, Stanground

Me And Dad

I was playing tennis outside with my dad
It started to rain and I got sad

Dad led me inside the house
I was as quiet as a mouse
I was soaking wet
But the fun wasn't over yet

It was still raining outside
Then Dad had an idea
He said we could play tennis inside the house,
But it wasn't a good idea
Anything could break into pieces
And Mum would pull Dad's ear

So we played in the hallway
Showing off too much
Then Dad was making the biggest shot of all
But he shot it so hard
It went so out of control

We were in shock
To see so many tiny window pieces
If Mum saw it she'd call the police
We'll be in so much trouble so Dad got the glue
And no one ever knew

Phew!

Daniel Read (14)
Stanground Academy, Stanground

Busta Rhyme - Expressions Of Youth

Trapped In School

School is like a prison
I haven't risen

There's coaches everywhere
And my mind's elsewhere

I am the leader of this rhyme
I hope what I said isn't a crime

The school is lame
I'm always to blame

I don't like this school
I think I'm too cool

I went to first aid
My pain didn't fade

They didn't say a thing
I feel like a king

They won't let me out
I give out a shout

There's too much homework
I'd rather play on the network

School is like a prison
And I still haven't risen.

Cameron (13)
Stanground Academy, Stanground

Gymnastics

It's my first gymnastics practise
I feel like I'm going to die from cactus

I ignore the feeling
And look at the ceiling

Then I walk into the gymnastics room
But the other girl faces gloom

Yeah I'm the new girl
But you're making my feet curl

Now let's start
I want to get smart

I'm getting good on the bars
While the other girls talk about guitars

Now it's my favourite part, the beam
And I'm also making friends with the team

Next is my floor routine
Gymnastics is almost over
Now I can get hot chocolate with cream

'How was your first day?' said Mum
I replied, 'It was lots of fun.'

Skye Chapman (12)
Stanground Academy, Stanground

Disappointed

Three years...
Three years waiting by the window
Dressed up
Packed up
Waiting as the wind blows

Finally for one special month
He came...
He looked just the same
My mum said that he was to blame
And that he put his name to shame

But I didn't care
I had plenty to share
I plaited my hair ready to go to the fair

We weren't alone
The social worker in our zone
I played, I laughed
But he thought I was daft
Sitting as I stayed alone

And that was it
We separated and split
I don't know why he came
But I feel I'm to blame.

Kenya Renshaw (13)
Stanground Academy, Stanground

My Brave Dog

My dog was very brave
She was my fave
I had her for thirteen years
And she helped me with all my fears
The day that she passed I couldn't hide my tears

When I was small I couldn't crawl
My dog picked me up
So I wouldn't fall

I wish that I could make her catch the ball
For one last time
I wish I could take her for a walk one last time
I wish I could hug her one last time
But that's not the rhyme

My dog was very brave
She was my fave
I had her for thirteen years
But now she's not near
And all I have are my tears...

Brandon Green (13)
Stanground Academy, Stanground

This Father's Day

I want to make it a special day
For my beloved dad
Out of all the dads in the world
He's one of a kind
I've made up my mind

Remember the day
When we both went to the restaurant
Or when I came to live at your's
I watched you as you did all the chores

Remember the day
When we both had tea
Or when we both had something to eat?

Remember the day
When we both went to the park
Or when we heard the dogs bark?

You're the best dad, you're not bad,
That's something I always remember!

Megan Cunningham (13)
Stanground Academy, Stanground

The Rain

As it drips
As it drops
I watch it all
As it pours

Sometimes I laugh
Sometimes I frown
Sometimes I wonder how long it'll last

Sometimes I think I'm a raindrop
Like me unable to stop

Sometimes I think I'm a bird
Like me flying so high, unable to be heard

Sometimes I think I'm the grass
Like me, different to the class

But then it rains
And I watch it again

Lost in my thoughts
Waiting to get caught...

Toby Lusher (12)
Stanground Academy, Stanground

Brother

My dear brother
You mean so much to me
No words can describe your cool vibe

My dear brother
I appreciate how much you do for me
Even when you change the channel when I watch TV

My dear brother
Times get hard but at least I've got you
To get me through

My dear brother
Even though you annoy me I do love you very much
You're a soft touch

My dear brother
You mean so much to me
No words can describe that what you do is amazing.

Megan Shire (13)
Stanground Academy, Stanground

Football Days

Football is the best
I love to beat the rest
We score all the goals and
Fulfil our happy souls

Ninety minutes kicking a ball
Players trying not to fall
Players running around
They can hear the sound of the crowd

The player goes in for attack
The other team start pulling back
He shoots, he scores
The crowd cheers and roars

The whistle is blown
The losing team begin to groan
Football is the best
I love to beat the rest.

Sam Cannizzaro (13)
Stanground Academy, Stanground

Christmas

Christmas, it's a great time of the year
Waking up in the morning and giving out a cheer
I waited for ages and it's finally here.

I open my presents and it's clear
I've been good this year
I say to myself with a sneer.

Christmas, it's a great time of the year
Eating mince pies
And seeing what everyone buys.

I finish my food and clear up my crackers
'I've been good this year,'
I say to my mum's ear.

Robbie Dowland (13)
Stanground Academy, Stanground

Just Me

My future isn't going to be like Macbeth
Or Romeo and Juliet
No...
No one's going to lure me
I know I'm the pure me
And if I'm not sure
I won't make a war

The witches can't show me
Who I'm going to be
They can't cure me
For I am free
I know I'm the free me but
No one can be me

I'm only me
But when I'm older...
My future will change me
And I can't wait to see...

Maisie Jean Goodley (13)
Stanground Academy, Stanground

My Best Friend

'Hi,' I said
To the back of the girl's head
She turned around and heard
What I said.

She is so kind
Hard to find
And I love her
We have the same mind

She doesn't have a Mr
But she has me as a sister
We have our aims
Because we're not the same

She is my best
And I am her rest
Together we are blessed

Our friendship is our test
But we're not stressed.

Bethany Perry (13)
Stanground Academy, Stanground

Love

Love is like a dove
It's something above
Someone to hug
With love

Love is like a smile
It's worth your while
Someone to make you laugh
With your half

Love is like trust
It's like gold dust
Some people lust
If they are fussed

Love is like happiness
It's a kind of madness
Some kindness
With lots of sweetness.

Jessica Bowman (12)
Stanground Academy, Stanground

Summer

I see something bright
I think it's the light
I open my eyes
And see the sunlight

So I put on my robe
And look at the rose
Then I sit on the chair
And do my hair

I open the door
And go outside
I see green trees
And lots of bees

I eat an ice cream
Which tastes like a dream
And enjoy the rest
Of this summer's best.

Oliwia Wiktoria Sliwinska (12)
Stanground Academy, Stanground

Time By Your Side

No matter how hard you try
Time will fly
It will pass you by
Just as you sigh.

No matter how quick you go
Time will go slow
It will pass you by
Just as you know.

No matter how much it hurts
Time will not divert
It will pass you by
Just as you exert.

No matter how
No matter when
Time will be there
See it as a friend.

Jenesis Smoot (13)
Stanground Academy, Stanground

Babies

Babies, they're all around me
That's why I'm an auntie
They're cute and noisy
Especially when they throw their toysies.

I have three nephews
One called Romeo
One called Preston
And one called Bentley
Oh how they love me!

My sister and I are close
Her sons care for me most
I love them all...
Here's a toast!

Alicia Gilbert (13)
Stanground Academy, Stanground

Father's Day

On Father's Day

I want you to remember the day I came
If you remember, it was you
Who gave me my name

We have our ups and downs
And I know how it sounds
But you're still my clown

I want you to remember the day I came
If you remember, it was you
Who gave me my name

And I love you the same.

Casey Sexton (12)
Stanground Academy, Stanground

You're Fab

Happy birthday Dad
I just want you to know
That you're fab!

I'm glad I have you in my life
And my mum - your wife
I know, when you flick my ears
This causes strife.

But regardless of everything
We share a sporting time,
I hope you enjoy reading this poem
From your son who rhymes.

William Lee Guy (13)
Stanground Academy, Stanground

Time

We all have time
It's like rhyme
It ticks, tocks every time.

We all have time
Like a bell that chimes
A reminder that's kinder

We all have time
Time to spend
And time to end

We all have time
It's our lifeline
That ticks, tocks every time.

Sam Bunczik (13)
Stanground Academy, Stanground

Favourite

I have three favourites,
They're all sci-fi,
They all have something,
That can fly high.

My third is Marvel,
My fave hero's Doctor Strange,
Then it is Vision
They both can do a range.

Avengers are amazing,
The Guardians are better,
The leader is StarLord,
And he killed his planet father.

The infinity war is of course,
The infinity stones and Thanos,
The old heroes will die,
The new ones will survive.

My second is Star Wars,
Where people use the force,
It has its own day too,
May the Fourth be with you.

Lightsabers are awesome
Common red, blue and green,
Mace Windu's is purple,
but isn't always seen.

Yoda, Qui Gonn,
Obi and Ani,
Maul, Dooku,
Vadar and Palpi.

My fave's Doctor Who,
13 doctors there's been,
Time machine's the TARDIS,
Time and relative dimension in space.

Eccleston, Tennant,
Smith and Capaldi,
Jodie Whittaker,
The next doctor will be.

The doctor's made enemies,
And many companions,
Enemies are the reason for
Most regenerations.

Jack Gourlay (13)
Thomas Adams School, Wem

Aggression

Aggressive people
With aggressive minds
Scurry around like children
Knowing not what the future holds
Hiding in a crooked block building.

What is the definition of normal, my dear,
And what on earth do you mean?
For when you do not tell me things
I fear for what may seem.

A lonesome boy
With lonesome genes
Lies to his lonesome mother
Whilst she herself is dying too,
On the inside but no other.

Why on earth would you help me so,
When I have done nothing for you
Except in November,
When you dolled up in splendour
And to that building you moved.

Clocks tick faster, faster, faster
And then stop altogether
You seem much too annoyed
To fix all these toys
So now infants must pester.

They are scared, frightened, terrified
But they all mean the same thing
And when they try to accuse you of such
You start to cry and then scream.

Why must you be this way,
Dear brother mine -
Why must you start like that?
Why must you side with another,
My dear,
For such an aggressive mind?

Evelyn Ross Platt (14)
Thomas Adams School, Wem

The War

The land, belonging to a great country,
Is now claimed by a battle,
A battle for each and everyone to be free.
The once farmer's field drowned in loss,
Loss of life, loss of hope, with souls hitting the floor,
Each stolen by the war.

Daffodils were bright yellow and blooming,
Now painted like a canvas in the crimson of blood,
The artist being war and the brushes being weapons,
The great field not so great any more,
The daffodils are no more,
Because they were stolen by the war.

The distant bombs and gunshots getting louder,
Louder as the land is consumed further by the battle,
Men and women drop into the flowers with wounds,
Wounds as bad as the battle itself,
Wounds that will never heal or mend,
Because the war will never end.

Charlotte Francis (13)
Thomas Adams School, Wem

I Thought You Were

Maybe it was clear, the look in your eye.
That way you grit your teeth when I'm behind.
Is it my fault? The bruises hide
nothing. I am stronger. If you think
I'll go down, hit me again. I'll show you.
What you cook up inside, it tastes good,
doesn't it? Then come back for more;
have another helping and soon I'll have dessert.
When you think I'm over, and you've ruined me,
I'll rub away the marks. Start again. This time
it will be different. I'll come back
with a fist in one hand and courage in the other:
I believe. The blood that runs through my veins
is heat and tiredness. Tired of you and of
myself, for not freeing myself earlier.

JJ Udy (12)
Thomas Adams School, Wem

Forget-Me-Not

For every rotting corpse,
A flower is planted.
It would fill a thousand fields,
Fields full of blooming roses
And lilies and tulips.
The ground would be littered with a rainbow of petals,
The air a sweet explosion of smells.
But will you forget -
Forget those who have died?
They died for you and me and everyone else.
He was shot with a gun.
She bled to death.
He drowned in a lake.
She spoke out too late.
Blood spatters the walls like a blooming rose,
A dead soul is beneath every flower that grows.

Freya Davies (13)
Thomas Adams School, Wem

Bricks

Bricks are solid,
Made from cement.
You can build houses
So you don't live in a tent.

Bricks can make structures,
Like a school.
Or the base
Of a swimming pool.

Bricks can hurt
If you fall on them,
But when they are placed,
Trees cannot stem.

Minecraft is fun,
Bricks are on that too.
I play it every day.
It can really inspire you.

Ben Gwilliam (13)
Thomas Adams School, Wem

Dream

We can be anything,
If we try.
Life isn't easy,
So why wait - to be something?

If we try,
We can succeed,
Put our heart,
To our dream,
Live happy,
To achieve!

Catherine Sutton (13)
Thomas Adams School, Wem

YOUNG WRITERS INFORMATION

We hope you have enjoyed reading this book – and that you will continue to in the coming years.

If you're a young adult who enjoys reading and creative writing, or the parent of an enthusiastic poet or story writer, do visit our website **www.youngwriters.co.uk.** Here you will find free competitions, workshops and games, as well as recommended reads, a poetry glossary and our blog.

If you would like to order further copies of this book, or any of our other titles, then please give us a call or visit **www.youngwriters.co.uk.**

Young Writers
Remus House
Coltsfoot Drive
Peterborough
PE2 9BF
(01733) 890066
info@youngwriters.co.uk